The Tale
of
Troubled Water

Written by Caleb Ocken

Illustrated by Moran Reudor

Archway Publishing books may be ordered through booksellers or by contacting:

Archway Publishing
1663 Liberty Drive
Bloomington, IN 47403
www.archwaypublishing.com
844-669-3957

Because of the dynamic nature of the Internet, any web addresses or links contained in this book may have changed since publication and may no longer be valid. The views expressed in this work are solely those of the author and do not necessarily reflect the views of the publisher, and the publisher hereby disclaims any responsibility for them.

Any people depicted in stock imagery provided by Getty Images are models, and such images are being used for illustrative purposes only.
Certain stock imagery © Getty Images.

ISBN: 978-1-6657-3670-1 (sc)
ISBN: 978-1-6657-3669-5 (hc)
ISBN: 978-1-6657-3668-8 (e)

Library of Congress Control Number: 2023900542

Print information available on the last page.

Archway Publishing rev. date: 01/11/2023

The Tale

of

Troubled Water

In a land where the drums would beat
To the rhythm of the heart,
Standing on shorelines of defeat,
A young boy is torn apart.
His name is Troubled Water

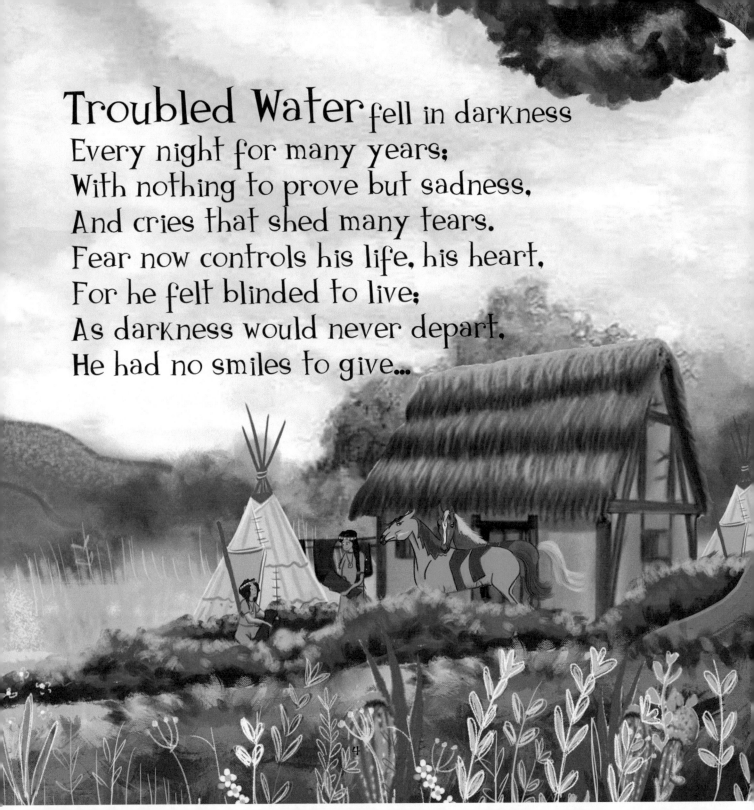

Troubled Water fell in darkness
Every night for many years;
With nothing to prove but sadness,
And cries that shed many tears.
Fear now controls his life, his heart,
For he felt blinded to live;
As darkness would never depart,
He had no smiles to give...

4

The tribe Troubled Water lived with
Prayed for the boy to be free;
Many attempts to solve his myth,
His darkness, no one could see...

6

Troubled Water was greeted by
The Great Tribe Mother of Love;
With an open mind and spirit,
The boy seeked help from above.

"Each night I pray for happiness,
Yet each day I wake in fear.
I have so much love to confess,
Yet Im so scared to be near."

The Tribe Mother saw the boys fright;
"Learning will help you to see.
Follow your heart into the light,
And your spirit shall be free."

9

"Like lightning in the dead of night,
Love helps our deepest wounds mend;
Like silence in a starry night,
Love will be our greatest friend."

"I have a quest for you, my son;
To discover who you are.
Into lands known only by Sun,
Become lost, and travel far."

"Each day shall bring lessons to hear,
So be silent and be true.
Even fear itself might appear,
So always believe in you."

That night the boy could barely sleep.
He was so ready to flee!
Before the Sun rose to its feet.
He left home, wild and free.

From his village, he would retreat
Before the others woke up:
Leaving with a quest to complete,
His Holy Grail to fill up.

14

And so begins a tale of love
Through the darkness of our heart;

15

The challenges we face above
Shall never tear us apart.

The boy traveled into his fate,
Until a great lake emerged.
Animals gathered to locate
With no intention to purge.

Tigers were kind, lions were fair;
And a surprise did he see,
Even he was allowed to share
Gifts of life and harmony.

18

That night as the stars danced around,
The young boy, Troubled Water,
Realized love makes the perfect sound;
A symphony through water.

19

Troubled Water woke to the sun
With no fears to keep him low.
The climb up the Mountains begun;
The Earth formed a steady flow.
Each step grew easy to give in,
The wind asked the trees to sway.
But at the peak felt like Heaven;
The Earth took his breath away.

That night as the stars blossomed out,
Troubled water soon felt free.
With knowledge flowing all about,
"Even Earth lives, Just like me.

23

The grass swayed as the wind would dance,
And animals came to play.
As for the boys fear, stood no chance
To disturb this happy day.

The Sun rose with an eager pace,
And the boy rose to his feet.
Down the mountain the boy would race
Into fields of corn and wheat.

That night as the stars sang aloud,
Troubled water lay with Joy.
Breathing fresh air creates a sound;
Music of life to enJoy.

27

Troubled water rose to the sun
As fire spread through the land.
He could not run, he could not hide,
But love gave a helping hand.
The tree line fell as the flame cracks,
Fear overwhelmed the boy's sight.
But nothing stopped him in his tracks;
Even death cant steal his light.

That night as the stars left a mark,
Troubled Water became bold.
Life that truly embraces dark
Will shine bright, hearts made of gold.

31

The sun was gone,
the smoke rose high,
And darkness cast to the light.
Troubled Water began to cry
As his fear danced with delight.
He screamed and fought, but could not see
That defeat is not the end.
He cried out "Nothing can stop me!
Love will always be my friend."

He closed his eyes, his heart open
To the world he never knew.
And with strength of one thousand men,
Troubled Water became new.
And the young boy dreamt away...

Visions of life from a distance;
The spirit of endless fun.
And the boy had no resistance
To join in with everyone.
Thoughts of love brought endless laughter
To resolve this inner fight.
For he knew from this point after,
Darkness could not take his might.

Troubled Water Jumped to his feet:
New discoveries were found.
Fear must always have a defeat
To begin tales we are bound.
And the boy was his strongest now,
Fear came swarming all around.
He screamed

"Nothing can fear me now!"
Darkness fled, and love was found.

The brave boy embraced the warm Sun
As the smoke clouds passed away.
His inner spirit had begun
To shine through his gloomy days.
His fear vanished, the sky turned blue;
And the land moved with pleasure.
For in his heart, the strong boy knew
Love is the greatest treasure.

That night the stars became alive;
Troubled Water cried with love.
"I've found my place here, on this Earth,
And in the Heavens above."
One amongst the stars...

The boy woke with the morning air,
And was sad to leave this source.
But he realized choices are there
For life to further its course.
He crossed valleys and plains and hills
Until home appeared below.
He had no fear to give him chills,
As family stood a-glow.

The young boy seeked out Tribe Mother
With spirits of elation,
To share all that he discovered;
His inner hearts foundation.

"Please sit," Mother said in soft pain,
"You have grown strong from your youth.
Accepting love will let you gain
Compassion, wisdom, and truth."

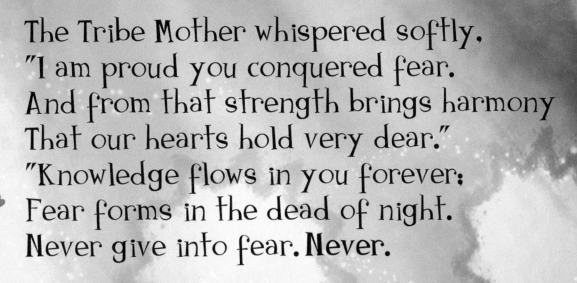

The Tribe Mother whispered softly,
"I am proud you conquered fear.
And from that strength brings harmony
That our hearts hold very dear."
"Knowledge flows in you forever;
Fear forms in the dead of night.
Never give into fear. Never.

Faith shall guide
you to the light"

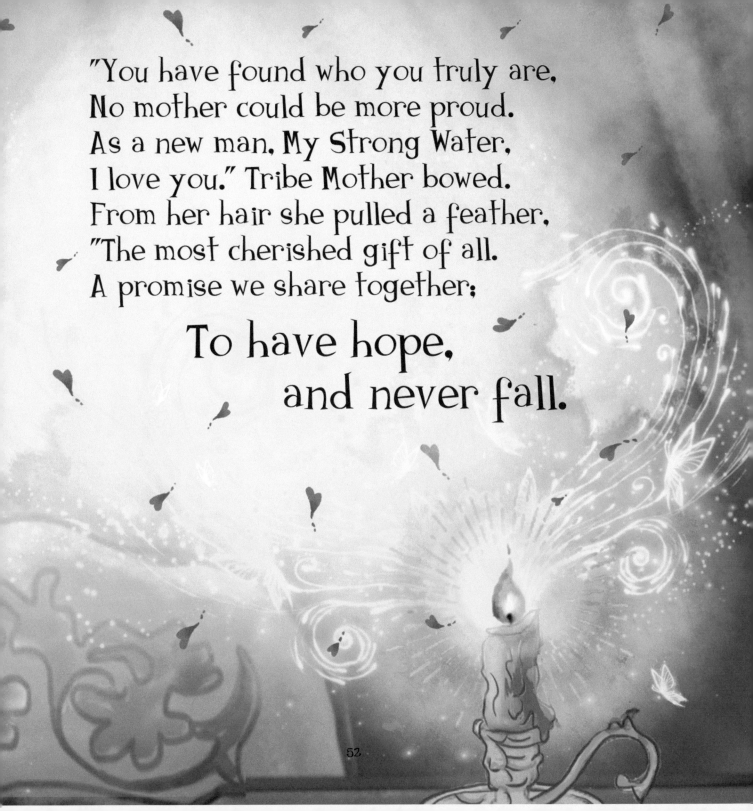

"You have found who you truly are,
No mother could be more proud.
As a new man, My Strong Water,
I love you." Tribe Mother bowed.
From her hair she pulled a feather,
"The most cherished gift of all.
A promise we share together;

To have hope,
and never fall.

"With this feather
I wish to share,
I must also be set free.
This body can
no longer bear
The Journeys set
before me."

53

"All beginnings must have an end,
For my Journey must end here.
But from my life, stories amend
As your Journey begins here."

Strong Water fought the urge to cry
"I cant do this on my own!
After blooming out like the sky,
How will my dim light be shown?"

"Stay strong my child" Mother hymned,
"This world may spin you around.
Just remember, no light is dimmed:
Stars of Heaven we are bound."

"I will always be here for you;
We share the love we call ours.
And every night when the Earth sleeps,

I'll be with you
in the stars..."

Leaving him with a kiss good-bye,
Mother traveled to the end.
And with the Sun, her holy guide,
Vanished to the sky. The End.

Printed in the United States
by Baker & Taylor Publisher Services